111

ANGEL MESSAGES

CHANNELED GUIDANCE
TO AWAKEN, HEAL & INSPIRE
YOUR SOUL

MICHELLE CLARE

ISBN: 979-8-9989292-3-6

DEDICATION

For the Angels, who have whispered, guided, comforted, and uplifted me through every moment of this life and beyond.

For my family and friends, your love is my anchor, my inspiration, and my reminder that we are never truly separate.

And for every soul who holds this book in their hands, may these messages awaken the knowing within you that you are never alone, that divine love surrounds you always, and that your angels walk with you in every step, every breath, and every chapter of your life. May these words be a spark of hope, a gentle healing, and a reminder of the infinite love that carries us all.

CONTENTS

INSPIRATION

From the very beginning, I want you to know this:
angels show up in many ways, and they are always closer
than you think. Sometimes they arrive as a soft whisper
of reassurance in your thoughts, or a comforting
warmth when you feel most alone. Other times they
appear through the smile of a loved one, the perfect
timing of a miracle, or even the unexpected kindness of
a stranger. Angels don't always come with wings and
halos—they come as love, showing up in the exact way
we need most. This book is a reminder of their
presence, their devotion, and the endless ways they are
supporting you right now.

1

The Best Version of You

Being the best version of yourself is a journey of continuous growth and self-discovery. It means embracing your strengths while acknowledging and learning from your weaknesses. It's about setting goals that align with your true passions and values, and striving each day to move closer to them. Being the best version of yourself requires courage to step out of your comfort zone, the humility to seek help when needed, and the resilience to bounce back from setbacks. It's a commitment to authenticity, to living a life that reflects your deepest beliefs and highest aspirations. When you dedicate yourself to this path, you not only transform your own life but also inspire those around you to do the same.

2

Embrace Your Shadow

Embracing your shadow is an essential journey towards wholeness and self-acceptance. This shadow represents the parts of ourselves that we often reject or hide, fearing they make us less worthy. Yet, within these hidden aspects lie profound truths and untapped strengths. By facing and embracing our shadow, we uncover the fullness of our humanity, integrating our light and dark sides into a balanced, authentic self. This courageous act of self-love allows us to heal, grow, and transform. It empowers us to live more authentically, with greater empathy and understanding for ourselves and others. Embrace your shadow, for it is a vital part of your journey to becoming your true, complete self.

3

Embrace Gratitude

Embracing gratitude transforms our perspective on life, revealing the beauty and richness in every moment. When we pause to appreciate the seemingly small things—the warmth of the sun, the kindness of a stranger, or the comfort of a familiar routine—we uncover a profound sense of contentment. Gratitude shifts our focus from what we lack to what we have, fostering resilience and joy. By cultivating a heart full of thanks, we enrich our lives with positivity and open ourselves to a deeper connection with the world and those around us. In every challenge and triumph, gratitude becomes the lens through which we see the extraordinary in the ordinary, turning each day into a gift.

4

*T*ake the Step

Sometimes, the smallest step you take can become the most pivotal moment in your life. It might seem insignificant, a mere whisper against the grand tapestry of your goals, but it holds immense power. By taking that step, no matter how modest it may appear, you set in motion a chain of events that can lead to extraordinary transformations. It's in those seemingly inconsequential actions that true progress begins.
So, embrace the courage to make that small move, for it could very well be the catalyst for your greatest achievements.

5

What is My Purpose?

"What is my purpose? What is my gift?" To be a force for love and kindness in this world is one of the greatest gifts you can offer. Every smile, kind word or compassionate gesture has the power to heal hearts and transform lives. In a world that often feels rushed and disconnected, your love becomes a sanctuary, a reminder that goodness still thrives. Kindness spreads like ripples in water, touching others in ways you may never see but can always trust. By choosing to lead with empathy and understanding, you become a light in the darkness, helping to shape a more gentle, caring world where others feel seen, valued, and loved.

6

Grief

Grief doesn't have a script; it moves in its own way and time, often surprising us with its depth and unpredictability. There's no set path to follow, no right or wrong way to mourn, and each person's journey through loss is as unique as the love they carry. Some days, the weight of it feels unbearable, and other days, moments of peace and joy quietly sneak in. It's messy, raw, and at times confusing. Grief has no timeline, no rules—it simply asks us to be gentle with ourselves as we learn to navigate life without the person, pet, place or thing we've lost, finding strength in the tenderness of our memories and the hope of healing.

7

Trust The Timing

Trust the timing of your life, for everything unfolds exactly when it's meant to. Sometimes, the waiting feels endless, and doubt creeps in, but the best things are worth that patience. Don't rush or settle for less than you deserve, because what's truly meant for you is on its way, even when you can't yet see it. Every delay, every closed door, is leading you closer to what aligns with your heart's deepest desires. Be patient with the process, knowing that your journey is shaping you into the person ready to receive all that you're destined for. Stay open, stay hopeful, and trust that what's meant to be will arrive at the perfect moment.

8

Let Go

There is a profound wisdom in letting go—a wisdom
that comes from understanding that holding on too
tightly can weigh us down. Letting go doesn't mean
giving up; it means trusting that what is meant for you
will come, and what is no longer serving you must
be released. It's a courageous act of faith, an
acknowledgment that some things, people, and
experiences are part of our journey for a season, not a
lifetime. In letting go, we create space for new growth,
new opportunities, and the peace that comes with
knowing that you are not defined by what you lose, but
by the strength and wisdom gained in the process.

9

The Web of Life

In the vast web of life, our connection to one another transcends physical space; we are linked by vibration, not location. It's the energy we emit—our thoughts, emotions, and intentions—that binds us together, creating invisible threads that stretch beyond the boundaries of time and space. Whether near or far, the vibrations we send out ripple through this web, touching the lives of others in ways we may never fully see. We are part of a greater whole, united by the shared frequencies of love, empathy, and understanding. In this way, our actions and feelings echo through the universe, reminding us that we are never truly alone, and that the connections we form with others are as powerful as the energy we bring to them. This is also how we are so beautifully connected to our loved ones in Spirit.

10

The Universe is Speaking

The Universe is always speaking to us, offering gentle whispers and signs to guide us along our journey. It communicates in the quiet moments, through synchronicities, intuitive nudges, and the unexpected encounters that touch our souls. Sometimes, it's a subtle reminder to pause, reflect, or change course; other times, it's a loud call to step into our purpose. The key is to listen, to trust that these messages are part of a greater plan, woven into the fabric of our lives to help us grow, evolve, and align with our highest selves. The Universe is constantly guiding us, if only we open our hearts and minds to its wisdom.

11

Honor Your Path

And if I could, I would go back and lovingly kiss each and every step along the path I have walked on my journey back to me. I would honor the moments of pain and confusion just as deeply as the times of joy and triumph, for every experience shaped who I am today. Each step—no matter how difficult or uncertain—was a part of my unfolding, guiding me closer to my true self. In every stumble and rise, I found strength and wisdom. And now, with deep gratitude, I see that even the hardest steps were filled with love, carrying me home to Myself.

12

Gratitude

Just for today, I will embrace gratitude with every breath. I will be thankful for each lesson learned, even those wrapped in pain, for they have shaped me into who I am. Every tear that fell was a testament to my strength, every moment of laughter a reminder of the beauty in life's simplest joys. I will cherish every hug that has warmed my heart and every smile that has brightened my days. Most of all, I will honor the gift of this moment, the opportunity to exist here and now, to feel, to grow, and to love fully.

And then I will try to do it again tomorrow and the day after that and the day after that...

13

Believe in What You Deserve

When you truly begin to believe in what you deserve, something incredible happens—you align your mindset with the possibilities around you. The energy you project shifts, opening doors you once thought were locked. Opportunities, connections, and blessings that seemed distant start flowing toward you because you're no longer settling for less. You realize your worth, and in doing so, you attract experiences and people that reflect that value. Confidence replaces doubt, and you become a magnet for abundance, joy, and growth. You'll be amazed at how much changes when you fully embrace the belief that you deserve the best life has to offer.

14

Bloom Where You Are Planted

No matter where life plants you, remember that your potential to grow and thrive is within you. It doesn't matter if the soil seems rocky or the surroundings feel unfamiliar—your ability to bloom is not limited by your circumstances, but created by the strength of your spirit. You carry a light that no one else can dim, a unique brilliance that can illuminate even the darkest of places. When you choose to shine where you are, you transform your environment, inspiring growth not only in yourself but in others. Embrace your power to bloom wherever you're planted, knowing that your light will always find a way to break through.

15

There is a Purpose

People enter our lives with purpose, even if we don't always see it right away. Some come for a reason, offering lessons, guidance, or support when we need it most. They might challenge us or help us grow in ways we never expected, but their presence is often temporary. Others come for a season, bringing joy, change, or companionship during a particular phase of our journey. They enrich our lives in specific moments but may leave as circumstances shift. Then there are those who stay for a lifetime, becoming anchors in our story. They walk with us through highs and lows, their bond with us growing deeper over time. Each person, whether they stay briefly or for the long haul, plays a role in shaping who we are, teaching us that every connection holds value, no matter how long it lasts.

16

New Possibilities

May each new sunrise fill your heart with hope, a gentle reminder that every day is a fresh beginning, full of possibilities waiting to unfold. As the first light touches the sky, let it awaken within you the belief that no matter what happened yesterday, today offers a new chance to grow, heal, and dream. And when the day comes to a close, may every sunset bring you peace, washing away the worries and burdens you may have carried. Let the fading light remind you that rest is just as important as striving, and in this quiet moment, may you find the comfort of knowing that you did your best. Trust that tomorrow will come with its own light, and in the space between, may your soul find calm.

17

*J*ust Breathe...

In this moment, let go of the weight you've been carrying. Trust that the universe is working behind the scenes, aligning everything in ways you can't yet see. There is a flow to life that moves with or without our constant worry. So breathe deeply, and surrender your fears and anxieties to the vast, loving wisdom of the universe. You are not alone in this journey—there is an energy greater than us, guiding you, protecting you, and bringing everything into place at the right time. Rest in that peace, knowing that you don't have to control it all. Simply breathe, and let the universe take care of the rest.

18

It's All Connected

Your gifts, your circumstances, your purpose, your journey, and your destiny. Every experience you've had, every challenge you've faced, and every talent you possess has been woven together to shape who you are becoming. Nothing is random; everything has meaning. Your gifts are not by chance—they are tools for your unique path. The obstacles you encounter aren't there to stop you, but to help you grow into the person you're meant to be. Embrace it all, even the uncertain moments, because they are molding you into the person you're destined to become. Trust that this journey, with all its twists and turns, is leading you exactly where you are meant to go.

19

*B*e *Grateful*

Be grateful for the life you have, for every moment of it has brought you to this point—your journey, with its highs and lows, is uniquely yours. Appreciate the love, the lessons, and the growth you've experienced along the way. While it's beautiful to dream and pursue the life you desire, never forget to honor the present. There's magic in the now, and every step you take is a bridge between what is and what will be. Gratitude grounds you, helping you see the blessings in the life you have, even as you work toward the future you envision. Trust that you can hold both—contentment and ambition—in your heart and still bloom into everything you're meant to be.

20

*T*he Best Day

The best day of your life is the one on which you decide that your life is truly your own. In that moment, you recognize that you have the power to shape your reality, make your own choices, and walk your own path. No longer do you need to apologize for who you are or make excuses for where you've been. You release the need to lean on others for validation, to rely on anyone for your happiness, or to place blame for what hasn't gone right. There is incredible freedom in taking full responsibility for your life—embracing both the victories and the setbacks as stepping stones on your journey.

This is the day your life really begins. From this point forward, you get to define what success, joy, and fulfillment look like for you. The gift of life has been handed to you, and it's an amazing, unfolding adventure, full of endless possibilities. Your perception and the narrative that you tell yourself will empower or disempower you. The quality of your life is in your hands, and with that, you have the power to create something beautiful, meaningful, and uniquely yours. Step boldly into this new chapter, knowing that you are capable of achieving all that your heart desires.

21

Turn The Page

It's time—turn the page and start a new chapter in life, embracing every possibility that lies ahead. The past has taught us, shaped us, and strengthened us but we are no longer bound by it. Be open and willing to step into a future that you have yet to explore. With renewed hope and purpose, it is time to release what no longer serves us, to let go of fears and doubts, and to welcome new experiences with an open heart. This new chapter is your chance to create, to grow, and to become more of who you truly are. Embrace it all—the challenges, the triumphs, the beauty, and the unknown—knowing that each step forward is a step toward becoming more of who you are meant to be.

22

Life is a Journey

Life is a journey of balance, a delicate dance between embracing challenges and finding peace within. Each moment offers a choice to grow, to let go, to forgive, and to love. When we align ourselves with our true essence, we allow the light within us to shine and connect with something greater than ourselves. This light guides us, reminding us that life's purpose is not to strive endlessly but to find harmony within the ebb and flow of each experience. Embrace the stillness, trust in the unfolding, and let the light flow through you, filling every step with grace, purpose, and peace.

23

*P*lay *Big*

This is no longer the timeline where you play small or dim your light. The world needs your brilliance, your unique gifts, and your authentic spirit now more than ever. Each experience, each lesson, has prepared you for this moment of stepping fully into who you are. Let go of past limitations and the voices that once held you back. You were meant to shine, to inspire, and to bring light to others. Embrace the power within you, knowing that you are capable of extraordinary things. This is your time to rise, to live boldly, and to make a lasting impact—no more holding back.

24

The Universe Has a Plan

The Universe's plan for you is more beautiful than anything you could dream of, unfolding in ways that surpass your wildest imagination. Trust that each step, even the ones that seem uncertain, is leading you toward something magnificent. There is a divine purpose woven into every experience, every challenge, and every moment of joy. While it may be hard to see the bigger picture now, know that you are being guided toward a life that is richer and more fulfilling than you could envision. Embrace the journey with an open heart, for the Universe has something extraordinary in store just for you.

25

It's a New Page

Every day is a new page, waiting to be filled with the actions and choices that can change your life. No matter where you've been or what yesterday looked like, today offers a fresh start, a chance to step closer to the dreams you hold. Every sunrise brings new opportunities, hidden in small decisions or bold moves, each one carrying the potential to lead you toward the life you truly desire. Embrace today with hope and courage, knowing that even the smallest shift can set you on a new path. You have the power to rewrite your story, one day at a time.

26

May Peace Prevail

Peace on Earth begins within each of us. When the world feels chaotic, remember that you are not powerless; true change starts inside. By choosing to seek inner peace, you lift your spirit and raise your vibration, becoming a beacon of calm in a turbulent world. As you find balance within, you anchor more light into the Earth, illuminating a path for others. Your peace radiates outward, touching lives in unseen ways and helping to bring harmony to the world around you. You are powerful. You are The Light, here to shine and bring hope.

27

Do Something That Truly Matters

If there was ever a moment to follow your passion and do something that truly matters to you, that moment is now. Life is too short to wait for the perfect time, the perfect conditions, or the approval of others. This moment is your invitation to step forward with courage, to embrace what lights up your soul, and to create a life that's meaningful to you. Your dreams are calling, and the world is waiting for the unique gifts only you can bring. Trust yourself, take that leap, and know that the time to start living fully, authentically, and with purpose is right now.

28

*B*e Unstoppable

Be unstoppable, for within you lies a divine light that is uniquely yours. Stand tall, knowing that your power comes from deep within—a strength that is unwavering and pure. Embrace the truth of who you are, and let that truth guide you forward, no matter what obstacles arise. Your light is meant to shine boldly, touching lives and inspiring change. Stand in your power with grace, knowing that every step you take with conviction brings you closer to the life you are meant to live. Believe in yourself, trust your path, and let nothing hold you back.

29

There Is No Finish Line

There is no finish line, no final destination to reach—
there is only the journey and the way you choose to
walk it. Life is a constant flow, always unfolding and
evolving, and you are the one who decides how to
respond. Each day offers choices: to grow, to adapt, to
savor the moment, or to change direction entirely.
Embrace this dynamic, knowing that it's not about
arriving somewhere, but about becoming more in tune
with yourself, more resilient, more compassionate, and
more true to who you are. Let go of the pressure to
reach some ultimate point and instead find joy in every
step, every lesson, every experience along the way.

30

Peace

May you find peace in each moment today, no matter how small or fleeting it may seem. Let the stillness of your breath, the warmth of a kind word, or the beauty of the world around you remind you that calm and serenity are always within reach. Even in the midst of chaos or uncertainty, may you discover those quiet spaces where your heart feels light and your mind feels free. Trust that every moment of peace you embrace today adds to the healing and strength within you, guiding you gently forward. You are deserving of this peace, and it is yours to claim, one moment at a time.

31

What If…

What if you realized how powerful you truly are? What if you understood that within you lies the ability to shape your reality, to overcome any challenge, and to inspire others simply by being yourself? You are more capable than you know, and every thought, choice, and action you take carries the potential to create waves of change. When you embrace your power, you step into your purpose, unleashing a strength that is both fierce and compassionate. Imagine what you could achieve if you trusted in your own light, knowing that you already have everything you need to rise, to grow, and to thrive. The world is waiting for the fullness of your power—believe in it, and let it shine.

32

Healing

Healing is an act of love you give to yourself, a quiet permission to let go of the pain that has anchored you in the past. It's not about erasing scars but embracing them as part of your journey, knowing they have shaped you but do not define you. Allowing yourself to heal means creating space for joy, forgiving yourself for being human, and choosing growth over stagnation. It's a tender process, filled with moments of courage and vulnerability, but each step forward opens your heart to the lightness of living fully. When you honor your healing, you reclaim your power and remind yourself that happiness is not a distant goal but a state you deserve right here and now.

33

Witness Yourself

Taking time to witness your own courage, strength, and beauty is one of the greatest acts of self-love you can offer. In the rush of life, it's easy to overlook how far you've come, the challenges you've faced, and the quiet resilience that has carried you through. Pause for a moment to truly see yourself—the courage it takes to keep going, the strength that has grown in every struggle, and the beauty that shines not just in how you look, but in how you love, care, and show up for the world. Acknowledging your own worth doesn't diminish anyone else's; it simply allows you to honor the remarkable person you are. You deserve to see yourself with the same admiration and kindness you so easily give to others.

34

*Y*ou Are Powerful

You are a powerful co-creator in this extraordinary journey called life, and every action you take is a brushstroke on the canvas of your dreams. Each day, do one thing—no matter how small—that moves you closer to the life you envision. Whether it's learning a new skill, speaking your truth, or simply believing in your own worth, these steps build momentum, turning intentions into reality. Trust that with every choice, you are aligning with the energy of creation, drawing your dreams toward you. The universe responds to your commitment and belief, and as you act with purpose and passion, you'll manifest a life that feels deeply aligned with your soul. Keep going—you're closer than you think!

35

Go Laugh

Go laugh in the places where your tears once fell, for
they are sacred markers of your growth. Go claim
victory where you once faced defeat, knowing that every
setback was a lesson in strength and perseverance.
Stand and shine boldly in front of those who doubted
you—not with bitterness, but with a heart full of love,
proving that your light cannot be dimmed by disbelief.
Rewrite your history with courage, turning pain into
purpose and doubt into determination. This is your life,
your journey—go live it fully, unapologetically, and
beautifully.

36

This Is Your Sign

Yes, this is your sign. Take the step! As the season begins to wrap up remember, new beginnings often bloom from the close of a chapter, reminding us that endings are not final but transformational. It's okay to feel unsure, to feel the ground shift beneath your feet—that's where growth begins. This is your chance to design a life that reflects your dreams, to walk a path that's uniquely yours. Embracing the unknown calls for courage, resilience, and an open heart—a willingness to trust in the beauty of what's yet to come. You are stronger than you realize and loved more than you know. Take the step, brave soul. The best is waiting for you.

37

*T*rue Growth

True spiritual growth unfolds not in the calm moments of meditation or the serenity of a yoga mat, but in the raw, unfiltered experiences of life's challenges. It emerges in the midst of conflict, when frustration, anger, or fear grips you tightly, tempting you to react as you always have. But then comes the realization—the profound awakening—that you hold the power to choose differently. This is where transformation takes root: in choosing patience over anger, understanding over judgment, and courage or love over fear. It's in these moments of choice, when you rise above your old patterns, that your spirit expands, and you step closer to the person you are meant to Become.

38

Be You

The vibration of being fully yourself and doing what you love is one of the most powerful forces in the universe. When you embrace your true essence and pour your heart into what lights you up, you radiate an energy that is undeniably magnetic. This energy not only draws the right people and opportunities into your life but also aligns you with a deeper sense of purpose and fulfillment. Trust that by living authentically and passionately, you are co-creating with the universe. Everything you need—support, abundance, and inspiration—will flow to you naturally when you honor who you truly are.

39

Answers

Answers often come not when we chase them
relentlessly, but when we find the courage to let go. In
our striving and overthinking, we sometimes create
noise that drowns out the quiet voice of clarity. But
when we release the need to control, to know
immediately, or to force solutions, we make space for
the answers to arise naturally. Letting go is an act of
trust—trusting in the timing of the universe and in the
wisdom within you. When you surrender, you shift
from resistance to flow, and in that stillness, the answers
you've been seeking often appear as if they were waiting
for you all along.

40

*Y*our *Journey*

Your journey here on planet Earth is sacred, a unique and extraordinary unfolding of your soul's adventure. Every experience—every joy, every challenge, every moment of stillness—is part of a divine tapestry that only you can weave. You are here for a reason, carrying gifts, lessons, and light that the world needs. Your existence is no accident; it is a miracle. Embrace the sacredness of your path, even when it feels uncertain, for it is in those moments of doubt and discovery that your spirit grows. Trust that you are guided, loved, and infinitely capable of making a difference simply by being who you are. This journey is yours, and it is your time to shine.

41

Have Peace

Have peace in your heart and mind, knowing that love is eternal and unbreakable. Close your eyes and take a deep breath. In the stillness, feel the presence of your loved ones in Spirit surrounding you. Their energy, their love, and their light are always with you, gently guiding and comforting you. Though they may no longer walk beside you in the physical world, their essence is woven into the fabric of your being. You carry them in your heart, in the memories that bring a smile to your face, and in the quiet whispers of encouragement you feel when you need it most. They walk beside you every day. Trust in the invisible threads of connection that cannot be severed by time or space. Your loved ones in Spirit are always near, sending you signs, wrapping you in love, and reminding you that you are never truly alone. Allow their presence to fill you with peace and gratitude, and know that their love continues to support you on your journey. In every quiet moment, when you open your heart, you can feel their gentle reassurance: "I am here, and I am with you always."

42

Permission

Give yourself permission to grow. I release past
versions of myself that no longer reflect who I am,
offering gratitude for all they've taught me. Those
earlier versions carried me through seasons of growth,
lessons, and challenges, but they are no longer who I
am. Today, I honor my evolution and embrace the
person I am becoming—stronger, wiser, and more
aligned with my truth. I am freeing myself to step fully
into the present, unburdened and ready to create a
future that reflects my highest self. With love
and compassion, I release what no longer serves me and
welcome all that awaits.

43

We Have Learned Enough from Pain

We have learned enough from pain, from the heartaches that have shaped us and the struggles that have tested our spirit. Pain has taught us resilience, compassion, and strength, but it's time to let love take the lead. It's time to embrace the lessons that love has to offer—the power of connection, the beauty of kindness, and the courage to open our hearts fully. Love teaches us to trust, to heal, and to see the good in ourselves and others. Let this be the season where we grow through joy, where love becomes the foundation of our choices, and where we learn that the most profound lessons are born not from suffering, but from the boundless gift of love.

44

Fall Deeply in Love

I hope you fall deeply in love with being alive—with the simple, miraculous act of breathing and existing. May you find wonder in the small moments: the warmth of sunlight on your skin, the sound of laughter echoing through a room, and the quiet peace of a sky full of stars. Let this be the year you rediscover the beauty in the everyday, where even challenges become stepping stones and setbacks reveal hidden strength. Fall in love with the possibility of each new day, with the power of hope, and with the gift of being present for it all. This year is yours to embrace, to cherish, and to live fully.

45

You Owe It to Yourself

You owe it to yourself to become everything you've ever dreamed of being, to honor the spark of greatness within you that refuses to dim. Every dream you hold close, every vision of the person you aspire to be, is a promise to yourself that deserves fulfillment. Don't let doubt or fear stand in your way—your potential is vast, your resilience unmatched. Take bold steps, even if they're small, and know that every effort brings you closer to the life you've imagined. You are worthy of success, joy, and purpose. The world needs the version of you that you dream of becoming, and more than anything, you owe it to yourself to see it through.

46

I Honor You

Through the challenges of life—the storms you've weathered, the trials that tested you, and the moments that felt impossibly heavy—you have emerged with a heart that remains kind. That is no small thing; it is an extraordinary act of courage. To love, to give, to care, even when the world has not always been gentle in return, is a testament to the strength of your spirit. And still, despite it all, you've held onto your compassion, your warmth, and your light. I honor you for that. I honor the quiet bravery it takes to keep believing in goodness and to continue offering it to the world. Your kindness is a gift, and it matters more than you know— it will ripple throughout eternity.

47

*P*lay Human

You came into this life to play human—to experience
the full, raw beauty of what it means to exist in a world
of contrasts. It's messy, unpredictable, and at times,
overwhelming, but that's the magic of it all. Your soul
chose to be here, at this exact time, knowing the
challenges you would face and the light you would
bring. Each moment of joy, heartbreak, confusion, and
clarity is part of your growth, shaping you into a
brighter, stronger version of yourself. You are here to
evolve, to learn, to feel, and to inspire. Even in the
darkest moments, your presence lights the way for
others, a reminder that life's contrasts are what make it
so extraordinary. You are a powerful soul, embrace the
journey—it's exactly where you're meant to be.

48

Move Forward

Sometimes, to move forward, we have to leave
something behind—a habit, a belief, a place, or even a
version of ourselves that no longer fits who we are
becoming. It's not easy to let go, especially when what
we're leaving is familiar or once brought us comfort.
But growth often requires release, creating space for
new opportunities, connections, and possibilities to
take root. Trust that what's meant for you lies ahead,
not behind, and that every step you take is a step toward
your evolution. Letting go isn't about loss; it's about
making room for something greater. The journey
forward begins when you choose to let go with grace
and courage.

49

Gifts, Talents & Perspectives

You have gifts that are uniquely yours—talents, perspectives, and abilities that no one else can offer in the way you can. But to share those gifts with the world, you may need to step outside your comfort zone. Growth often begins at the edge of familiarity, where uncertainty meets opportunity. It might feel intimidating at first, but every step you take into the unknown is a step toward fulfilling your potential. Trust that your gifts are needed and that the world is waiting for what only you can provide. Embrace the challenge, for it is in those moments of courage that you truly shine.

50

Divine Timing

Our lives are beautifully guided by divine timing, unfolding exactly as they are meant to, even when we can't yet see the bigger picture. Trust that what is meant for you—the people, the opportunities, the experiences—will find you at the perfect moment. You cannot miss what is divinely aligned for your journey. When doors close, it's not rejection but redirection; when delays happen, they're often preparing you for something greater. Surrender to the flow of life, knowing that every step, even the uncertain ones, are leading you toward your highest good. What is yours will never pass you by.

51

Look Inward

When we are no longer able to change a situation, life invites us to look inward and find the strength to change ourselves. This is a call to grow, to adapt, and to transform in ways we never imagined. It's in these moments of surrender that we discover our true power—the power to shift our perspective, to let go of what no longer serves us, and to create a new path forward. Change within doesn't mean giving up; it means rising up, becoming resilient, and choosing to evolve. When the external world feels immovable, know that the greatest change always begins within you, and from that inner transformation, a new reality can unfold.

52

A New Opportunity

Every day is a new opportunity—a blank canvas waiting for you to paint your story. No matter what yesterday held, today offers you the chance to begin again, to try something new, to take a step closer to the life you dream of. Each sunrise brings fresh hope, new lessons, and the possibility to grow, heal, and create. It's a reminder that nothing is set in stone and that every moment is an invitation to embrace your potential. Today is yours to shape, to fill with kindness, courage, and intention. Seize it with an open heart, knowing that every small step forward is a beautiful act of becoming.

53

Never Be Afraid to Soar

Never be afraid to soar—you were built to fly. Within you lies limitless potential, a spirit designed to rise above fear, doubt, and anything that tries to hold you back. The sky is not your limit; it is your invitation. Trust your wings, embrace your journey, and know that every challenge is just a gust of wind lifting you higher. You were never meant to stay grounded in fear—you were meant to spread your wings and soar beyond anything you ever imagined.

54

What Would You Like?

At its core, this question is rooted in life's simplest yet most profound inquiry: What would you like? Our desires are not trivial—they are the sparks that connect us to the infinite potential of life itself. When we dare to embrace what we want, we open ourselves to growth, to adventure, and to transformation. Life expands as we reach for it, and in turn, we expand alongside it. So, take a moment to dream, unburdened by the fear of failure. Imagine a life where anything is possible, where the pursuit of your desire is not a risk but a certainty. What would you like? What would you create? The answer is waiting to unfold, as limitless as the universe itself.

55

Time To Shine

May you always feel the unconditional love and support of the Universe, guiding you toward your highest good Trust that you are never alone, that every challenge is shaping you, and that every step forward is a testament to your strength. Choose to believe in yourself, to honor your dreams, and to walk your path with courage. The Universe conspires in your favor—believe it, embrace it, and let your light Shine.

56

You Are Powerful

When you come out of the storm, you won't be the same person who walked in—that's the very purpose of the storm. It may shake you, challenge you, and even break parts of you that were never meant to stay. But within the chaos, you will find strength you never knew you had, resilience that refuses to fade, and a deeper understanding of who you truly are. The storm is not here to destroy you; it is here to transform you. And when the skies clear, you will emerge wiser, stronger, and more radiant than before—carrying with you the lessons, the growth, and the unshakable truth that you were always meant to rise. You are an unstoppable and powerful soul.

57

You Are Always Connected

The spiritual world, though unseen by most, is a vast, infinite realm that connects us to an unlimited consciousness—one without edges, boundaries, or limits to what it can create. It is the space where divine wisdom flows, where possibilities are endless, and where the answers we seek already exists. When we open our hearts and minds to this higher plane, we tap into a source of love, guidance, and creativity far beyond what the physical world can offer. Trust that you are always connected to this boundless energy, and within it, you have the power to create, to heal, and to become everything you were meant to be.

58

Letting Go

Letting go is not about weakness or surrender—it is the ultimate act of self-love and freedom. When you release the pain, the resentment, the regrets that weigh you down, you open yourself up to a future unburdened by the past. It is not about forgetting but about choosing peace over pain, growth over stagnation. Holding on keeps you trapped in a cycle that no longer serves you, but letting go is the gift you give yourself—the permission to heal, to move forward, and to embrace the life that is waiting for you. You deserve that freedom. You deserve to step into your future unchained.

59

Perception

The power of perception may seem small, but it shapes your entire world. The way you choose to see a challenge determines whether it defeats you or strengthens you. A setback can be a sign of failure or a lesson in resilience—it all depends on how you perceive it. When you shift your perspective, you shift your reality. What once felt impossible becomes an opportunity, what once hurt you becomes a stepping stone. The world doesn't change, but how you see it does, and that changes everything. Your perception holds the key to your happiness, your growth, and your ability to rise beyond every limitation.

60

Be Love in Action

Be love in action—not just in words or feelings, but in the way you show up for the world. Let love be the driving force behind your kindness, your patience, your willingness to lift others up. Love is not passive; it is a choice, a commitment, a way of being. It's in the way you listen with empathy, offer a helping hand, or simply smile at a stranger. When you embody love, you become a source of light, reminding others of their own worth and goodness. Every act of love, no matter how small, creates a ripple that can change lives—including your own.

61

Release With Ease

May you release, with ease, what has passed, honoring it for the lessons it brought, yet freeing yourself from its weight. Like the trees that shed their leaves in trust of new growth, you, too, can surrender the past with grace. Turn your heart toward the present, where fresh dreams and untapped potential begin to stir. Gently tend to what is flowering within you—your passions, your purpose, your evolving self—nurturing each bud of possibility with patience and love. It is time for you to step into your season of abundance, to prepare to bloom and prosper, knowing that all you need is already within you, waiting for the light of your own belief.

62

*Y*ou *Are Unstoppable*

You have fire in your soul—a light that cannot be dimmed, a strength that refuses to be broken. It is the passion that fuels your dreams, the resilience that lifts you when life tries to push you down, and the courage that dares you to rise again and again. This fire within you is your power, your truth, your unshakable spirit. Let it burn brightly, igniting your purpose and lighting the way forward. Never shrink, never doubt—trust in your inner fire, and watch as it turns obstacles into stepping stones and dreams into reality.

You are Unstoppable.

63

New Possibilities

You are here, and because of that, the world holds new
possibilities. A new trajectory is always within reach,
waiting for you to claim it. It all begins with your
thoughts—the seeds of change, the whispers of
possibility and the new dreams you are dreaming, When
you choose thoughts of strength, hope, and purpose,
they transform into emotions that fuel your spirit.
Those emotions then become actions, and actions shape
your future. This is how legends are made—not by
waiting, but by believing, feeling, and boldly stepping
forward. You have the power to create, to shift, to
inspire. Trust in your ability to shape your own
path, and watch as the world rises to meet you there.

64

Repeat After Me

I am powerful, wise, strong, and capable—I hold everything I need within me to navigate this life with confidence and grace. No challenge is too great, no obstacle too strong, because I am resilient and resourceful. Wisdom flows through me, guiding my decisions and lighting my path. Strength lives in my soul, lifting me in moments of doubt and pushing me forward with determination. I trust myself, I believe in my abilities, and I know that I am more than able to rise, grow, and thrive. No matter what comes my way, I stand firm in the truth of who I am—I am unstoppable.

65

Focus

Right now, your focus should be on holding the light—
on choosing hope, kindness, and love even in the face
of uncertainty. By cultivating peace within yourself, you
become a beacon for others, radiating calm in a world
that often feels chaotic. Every thought, every action,
every moment of inner stillness contributes to the
greater whole, helping to shift collective human
consciousness toward a higher vibration. Change begins
within, and as you nurture light and peace in your own
heart, you inspire others to do the same. Together, our
energy can transform the world—one mindful, loving
intention at a time.

66

Connect Within

To navigate life for your highest good, you must first be deeply connected to yourself. Your inner world—your intuition, emotions, and true desires—holds the wisdom you need to move forward with clarity and purpose. When you are in tune with yourself, you make choices that align with your soul, rather than being swayed by external noise or fleeting expectations. This connection is your guiding light, leading you toward growth, joy, and fulfillment. The more you nurture this relationship with yourself, the more effortlessly life unfolds in harmony with your highest path. Trust yourself— everything you need is already within you.

67

Becoming

Stop shrinking to fit places you've outgrown—whether it's relationships, environments, or versions of yourself that no longer serve you. Growth is meant to expand you, not confine you. When you dim your light to make others comfortable or stay in spaces that no longer align with your soul, you deny yourself the fullness of who you are meant to become. Trust that outgrowing something isn't a loss; it's a sign of evolution. Give yourself permission to step boldly into the new, into the unknown, into the spaces that match the person you are becoming. You weren't meant to fit in—you were meant to rise.

68

The True Gift

The true gift of life isn't what we achieve—it's who we become through life's challenges. Every struggle shapes us, awakening strength, wisdom, and resilience. Hardships aren't meant to break us but to reveal our highest potential. The real treasure isn't the destination—it's the transformation. Embrace the journey, and you'll discover that the greatest reward is the evolved, radiant soul you become along the way.

69

Embrace The Unknown

Embrace the unknown, for it is where life's magic
unfolds. Some of the most beautiful chapters of your
journey won't reveal their meaning until much later.
Trust that even in uncertainty, you are being guided
toward something greater than you can yet see. The
moments that feel unclear now may one day be the ones
that shaped you the most. Let go of the need for every
answer and allow life to surprise you. One day, you'll
look back and realize that the chapters you once
questioned were the very ones that made your story
extraordinary.

70

Choice

Each day, we stand at a crossroads, presented with a profound choice: to build our lives on the foundation of love or to succumb to the constraints of fear. Choosing love empowers us to craft a life filled with purpose, joy, and connection, while fear often leads to regret and missed opportunities. By embracing love over fear, we unlock the potential to design a life that not only fulfills us but also radiates positivity to those around us. Remember, the power to choose lies within you; let love be your guiding compass.

71

Change

Change is an integral part of our spiritual journey,
serving as a divine invitation to evolve and align
more closely with our true selves. By embracing change,
we allow ourselves to be guided by higher wisdom,
trusting that each transformation brings us closer to our
intended path. Recognizing that change is inevitable, we
can choose to approach it with a willingness to grow,
understanding that through change, we are offered
opportunities for deeper development. By surrendering
to the flow of transformation, we open our hearts to the
boundless possibilities that await, allowing the divine to
work through us in creating a life of fulfillment.

72

Discernment
Not Everything that Comes Back is Meant to Stay

In life's journey, familiar patterns or individuals may reappear, evoking nostalgia or unresolved emotions. While these returns can offer opportunities for reflection and growth, it's essential to discern their purpose in your current path. Not everything that comes back is meant to stay; some reappearances serve as gentle reminders of lessons learned, while others test our readiness to move forward. Embrace these moments with gratitude, acknowledging their role in your evolution, and trust your inner wisdom to guide you in deciding what aligns with your highest good. By doing so, you honor your journey, welcoming what serves you and gracefully releasing what no longer contributes to your spiritual growth.

73

*T*he Light

May you awaken each day with the awareness that light surrounds you, even in the darkest moments. May you come to recognize that this same light lives within you—divine, radiant, and eternal. It is the essence of your soul, the spark of your purpose, and the truth of who you are. As you honor this light within, may you have the courage to let it shine boldly and unapologetically. Let your presence be a beacon of hope, healing, and love in the world. For when you shine your light, you give others permission to find and share theirs too—and together, we illuminate the path Home.

74

Wisdom and Understanding

Wisdom lives in the quiet spaces between words, in the stillness where the mind softens and the soul begins to speak. It is not always found in books or noise, but in the sacred hush where truth reveals itself. True understanding is more than information—it is a knowing that rises from within, beyond logic, beyond explanation. It's the deep resonance you feel when your heart recognizes something timeless and true. In silence, we remember who we are. In stillness, we connect with the Divine. And in that connection, wisdom blooms— not from what we've been told, but from what we've come to know in the depths of our being.

75

*T*he Past

Don't let the weight of the past steal the beauty of this moment. Right here, right now, is where your life is unfolding. The present is not just a passing second—it is a gift, a sacred opportunity to breathe, to feel, to begin again. Whatever has happened before does not define you; it has only prepared you for the depth and richness of this moment. Don't miss it looking backward. Your power, your peace, your joy—they live here, in the now. Embrace it fully, with open hands and an open heart, because this moment is your life… and it's worth showing up for.

76

Sacred Places

There are two sacred places your soul longs to return to again and again. The first is the place that heals you—the quiet space where your heart can exhale, where you remember who you are beyond the noise and the wounds. It might be nature, stillness, prayer, or the arms of someone who sees you clearly. Go there often, and let it restore you. The second is the place that inspires you—the space that awakens your spirit, stirs your dreams, and reminds you of what's possible. Whether it's a creative spark, a sunrise, or a bold idea, return to it with intention. Between these two places, you'll find your strength, your clarity, and the path Forward.

77

Courage

May you have the courage to break the patterns in your life that no longer serve your soul. May you look gently but honestly at the cycles that keep you small, the habits that dim your light, and the stories that no longer speak your truth. Change is not always easy, but neither is staying stuck in a life that doesn't reflect who you are becoming. Trust that you are strong enough to let go, to choose differently, and to rise. With each brave step away from what no longer serves you, you create space for healing, expansion, and the life your spirit truly desires.

78

*B*e Fully Present

May you be fully present today, grounded in this moment, where life is quietly unfolding its miracles. As you focus on your breath, let each inhale remind you that you are alive, and each exhale release what no longer serves you. In the stillness, may you find the beauty that often goes unnoticed—the warmth of light, the whisper of peace, the simple grace of being. Life is offering you gifts today: a fresh perspective, a gentle nudge, a moment of clarity. Be here for it. Receive it all with an open heart, for the present is where your power and your peace live.

Gratitude

I am deeply grateful for the quiet moments – the sacred pauses where time seems to slow and the world softens. In those still spaces, I meet myself fully. Without distraction or noise, I can hear the gentle wisdom of my soul, feel the steady pulse of life in my breath, and sense the quiet grace that holds me. These moments don't demand performance or perfection; they simply invite presence. And in that presence, I've discovered a deeper kind of peace – the kind that doesn't need explanation, only acknowledgement. It's in the quiet that I remember who I am beneath the noise and reconnect with the beauty that so often hides in plain sight. I'm equally grateful for the moments when my heart shattered – those tender raw spaces that once felt like endings. They taught me the language of resilience and broke me open in the most sacred way. Through the cracks, light found its way in, and with it came compassion, humility, and a richer capacity for joy. I now hold life more gently, more reverently, knowing how quickly it can change. Every beautiful moment – every smile, sunrise, and act of love – feels more precious because of the pain that shaped me. My heart may have broken, but it rebuilt itself wiser, softer, and wide open to the wonder of it all.

80

Uprooted

Life has a way of uprooting us—sometimes gently, often suddenly—pulling us from the familiar and casting us into storms we never saw coming. In the chaos, what we once knew may crumble. The structures, identities, and rhythms we built around us can fall apart like sand in the wind. It can feel like destruction, like an undoing of everything solid. And yet... beneath the wreckage, life still pulses. Quietly. Unshakably. Because there is only life—it does not stop, even in grief, death or uncertainty. It rebuilds, renews, rises through the cracks. And so will you. What was deconstructed will become sacred ground for something more aligned, more true. The storm is not the end. It's the clearing. Life always finds a way forward—and so will you.

81

Your Soul

Your soul is a sacred seeker—forever reaching, learning, evolving. It didn't come here to stay comfortable or untouched by challenge; it came to grow, to stretch, to remember its own divine light. Within you is a deep longing not just for answers, but for transformation— for wisdom that only experience can offer. Every joy, every ache, every moment of uncertainty is part of that journey, guiding you home to your truest self. Trust that your soul knows the way. It is not lost; it is expanding. And in every step forward, even the uncertain ones, you are becoming more of who you were always meant to be.

82

What Do You Desire?

What is it that you truly desire for your future—peace, purpose, love, or a life that feels deeply aligned with your soul? Everything you long for is already on its way to you, waiting for your belief, your vision, and your commitment to become who you're meant to be. The future isn't some far-off place—it's being shaped by your thoughts, your choices, and your energy right now. What you dream of is not out of reach; it's ahead of you, calling you forward. So, trust the path, stay rooted in your vision, and move with intention. The life you desire is already unfolding—you're not chasing it, you're stepping into it.

83

Focus on the Lesson

Focus on the lesson, and you will continue to grow. Life is always speaking to you—through every challenge, every joy, every unexpected turn. When you shift your attention from the pain to the wisdom it carries, you begin to rise above the moment and step into your power. Growth doesn't always come from comfort—it often blooms from discomfort, from reflection, from choosing to learn instead of resist. The more you embrace the lessons, the stronger, wiser, and more aligned you become. Trust that nothing is wasted. Every experience is shaping you into the person your soul came here to be.

84

You're not Late

You're right on time—divinely timed, perfectly placed, and exactly where you need to be. The delays, the detours, the moments you questioned your path—they weren't wasted. They were preparation. They were shaping your strength, refining your vision, and deepening your purpose. Your journey is sacred, and it was never meant to look like anyone else's. Don't measure your becoming against someone else's timeline. Trust the rhythm of your own soul. The unfolding of your life is a masterpiece in progress, and every step is leading you to where you're meant to be. Keep going—you are right on time.

85

Becoming You

This part of your life is not an ending—it's a sacred rebirth. You are shedding old layers, outdated beliefs, and versions of yourself that no longer reflect your truth. It may feel unfamiliar, even uncomfortable, but that's what transformation feels like. You are not lost—you are being reintroduced to who you truly are beneath the noise, the expectations, and the past. This is your awakening, your return to authenticity. Trust the unfolding. The pieces are not falling apart—they are falling into place, revealing the radiant, powerful soul you were always meant to be. You are not becoming someone new—you are finally becoming you.

86

Transformation

There's a quiet, sacred beauty in the in-between—the space where clarity hasn't fully arrived, but something deep within you is already shifting. It's the pause between what was and what will be, where you may not see the whole path, yet your soul is expanding with every uncertain step. Don't rush through it. The in-between is where growth takes root, where unseen miracles begin to bloom. Trust that even without all the answers, transformation is happening. You are being prepared, refined, and aligned for what's next. This is not a waiting room—it's a becoming.

87

Take The Step

You may never feel 100% ready—and that's okay.
Growth rarely shows up wrapped in certainty. The truth
is, most of life's most beautiful breakthroughs begin
with a shaky first step, not a perfect plan. If you wait for
the perfect moment, the flawless confidence, the
complete clarity, you might be waiting forever. But
when you choose to move forward anyway—despite the
doubt, despite the fear—you awaken your courage, and
that's when the magic begins. Trust that you are more
prepared than you realize and let your faith be louder
than your fear. Do it anyway—your future is waiting on
the other side of that leap.

88

Self-Love

Self-love is the lesson that comes dressed in a thousand forms—sometimes as heartbreak, other times as solitude, boundaries, forgiveness, or the quiet courage to choose yourself. It arrives not just in the gentle moments, but in the ones that break you open and ask you to remember your worth. It teaches through every "no" that honors your peace, every tear that waters your growth, every choice that says, "I matter." Self-love is not a single act—it's a sacred practice, a return to your own heart over, and over again. And when you embrace it, you don't just heal—you rise.

89

Choose to Rise

Even in the heaviness of grief, in the ache of hard times, and the noise of a chaotic world, you still hold one undeniable power—the power to choose who you become. Storms may rage around you, but they cannot touch the core of your spirit unless you let them. You can choose to harden, or you can choose to soften. You can crumble, or you can rise. Even when life feels unfair and the path unclear, your soul knows the way. Let this be your reminder: your power isn't in controlling the chaos—it's in how you meet it. Choose love over fear, courage over comfort, truth over silence. Choose to rise—not in spite of the world, but because you were born to be a light within it.

90

Moving On

Moving on is not a setback—it's a step forward in your evolution. Every experience, every lesson, every moment of growth has shaped you into someone stronger, wiser, and more aligned with your truth. You're not starting over; you're starting from a higher level, carrying with you the insight, resilience, and clarity you've earned along the way. The path ahead may be new, but you're walking it with a deeper understanding of who you are and what you deserve. Trust that moving on isn't losing ground—it's rising into the next chapter of your becoming.

91

Let It Go

Let it go—not because it didn't matter, not because it didn't hurt, but because you matter more. Carrying pain, resentment, or what-ifs only weighs down your beautiful, becoming soul. You are not meant to live anchored to what broke you. You are meant to rise, to heal, to breathe freely again. Letting go is not forgetting—it's honoring your worth enough to make space for peace. It's choosing your joy over your wounds, your future over your past. Release it, not as a sign of weakness, but as the greatest act of love you can offer yourself. You deserve that freedom.

92

Soulmates

Soulmates aren't limited to one person or one love story—we are gifted with many throughout our lifetime. They arrive as friends who feel like home, family members who see our soul, romantic partners who awaken us, and even as the animals who love us without condition. Each one comes with a purpose: to help us grow, to remind us who we are, and to walk beside us as we heal and evolve. Your true soulmate won't complete you—they will reflect your wholeness, encourage your light, and inspire a deeper love for yourself. Their presence will feel like alignment, not effort. You'll know them not just by how they love you, but by how peacefully you love yourself when you're with them.

93

You Are Ready

I'm sending you waves of courage—the kind that stirs deep within your soul and reminds you that you are worthy of a life that reflects your highest good. It takes strength to recognize the patterns that have kept you small, and even greater bravery to break them. But you are ready. You are ready to release what no longer serves you, to honor the whisper within that says, there is more for you. Trust that every step you take toward freedom, toward authenticity, is a step into the life your spirit has been longing to live. You are not alone in this transformation—grace is walking with You.

94

Be You

The vibration of being fully who you are and doing what you love is pure magic. It's magnetic, drawing to you the people, opportunities, and blessings that match your truest frequency. When you live in alignment with your heart, you don't have to chase what's meant for you—you simply become a beacon for it. Trust that by standing in your authenticity and following what lights you up, you are already calling in everything you need. The universe responds to truth, to passion, to joy—and when you embody that energy, life aligns in ways more beautiful than you could ever imagine.

95

*Y*our Path

You are here to carve out a new way of walking through life—not just for yourself, but for all those who will come after you. With every brave step you take into the unknown, every old pattern you break, and every dream you dare to honor, you are lighting a path where there was none before. Your courage to live differently, to trust your soul's wisdom over the world's noise, becomes a living invitation for others to believe in their own possibilities. You are not just creating a life—you are creating hope, inspiration, and a new way of being. And because of your journey, others will see that they, too, can rise.

96

Every Decision

Every decision you make is a brushstroke on the canvas of your life. By asking yourself, "Does this support the life I am trying to create?" you align your actions with your deepest aspirations. This simple yet powerful question serves as a compass, guiding you toward choices that resonate with your true purpose. Embracing this mindset empowers you to move forward with clarity and intention, transforming your dreams into reality. Remember, the life you envision is not a distant destination but a path you forge with each deliberate step.

97

Today

Today, give yourself permission—to rest, to heal, to be authentically you. Embrace the power to say no, to change, to love yourself unconditionally, to ask for help, to make mistakes, to pursue your dreams, and to live, play, laugh, and love. Recognize that granting yourself this permission is not a luxury, but a necessity for your well-being and growth. By honoring your needs and desires, you create a life that reflects your true self and opens the door to endless possibilities. Embrace this journey with compassion and courage, knowing that you are worthy of all the joy and fulfillment life has to offer.

98

Healing

Healing doesn't mean the damage never existed; it means the damage no longer controls your life. Healing is a breakthrough—an inner revolution where you rise beyond the pain that once held you captive. It's about acknowledging your wounds without allowing them to dictate your present or future. It's in this sacred breaking open that you reclaim your power, ignite your resilience, and begin to grow in ways you never imagined. Every step forward becomes proof of your strength, every scar a symbol of your triumph. Healing isn't just recovery—it's your soul's breakthrough into freedom, wholeness, and light.

99

Alignment

Aligning yourself with beliefs that serve you is one of the most powerful acts of self-love. When you choose thoughts rooted in possibility, worthiness, and truth, you begin to reshape your reality from the inside out. No longer bound by old stories or limiting patterns, you open yourself to a life that reflects your highest potential. The beliefs you hold become the compass that guides your choices, your energy, and your destiny—so choose ones that uplift, empower, and remind you of who you truly are: limitless, radiant, and deeply worthy everything good.

100

One Powerful Choice

All it takes is one powerful choice—one bold, soul-led decision to step into the life you truly desire. In that moment, the Universe responds. Energy shifts. Doors you couldn't see before begin to open. The right people cross your path. Opportunities align with divine precision. It's not about having it all figured out—it's about choosing with intention, with faith, with the knowing that your decision sets powerful forces into motion. That single moment of clarity can become the spark that changes Everything.

101

*T*ime to Shine

Daring to be the real you is the adventure of a lifetime—a courageous act of soul that calls you to rise, to shine, to live fully and unapologetically. You weren't born to dim your light or shrink to fit someone else's story. You came here with purpose, with fire, with gifts the world has never seen before in quite the same way. Every time you choose authenticity over approval, truth over fear, you awaken something powerful within. This life isn't about playing small—it's about boldly becoming all that you are and embracing the extraordinary journey that unfolds when you do. It is time to rise and let yourself shine!

102

Open Your Heart

The more grateful you are for what's here—the small joys, the hidden blessings, the lessons wrapped in everyday moments—the more your heart opens to receive what's coming. Gratitude is a sacred magnet for miracles; it tells the Universe, "I see the beauty, I honor the journey, I'm ready for more." When you fully embrace the present with love and appreciation, you naturally align with a future that reflects that same energy. What's meant for you begins to flow with grace, because you've made room for it through the simple, powerful act of giving Thanks.

103

*Y*our Soul's Divine Plan

You are here on purpose, with purpose—woven into this world with divine intention. Every heartbeat, every breath, every twist in your journey is not random, but part of a greater design calling you to rise into who you truly are. You carry a light no one else can shine, a voice no one else can speak with, and a soul that was chosen for this time, this place, this mission. Even in moments of doubt, trust this truth: you were made for something meaningful, something sacred. The Universe doesn't make mistakes—you are here to awaken, to impact, and to radiate the purpose that only you can fulfill.

104

Message From Your Guardian Angel

I am so deeply proud of you—watching you rise, heal, and choose to love and live again has been nothing short of awe-inspiring. Your courage to reopen your heart after pain, to find beauty in life again, and to trust in the goodness of what's still possible speaks to the strength of your soul. You've turned your wounds into wisdom, your grief into grace, and your journey into a powerful testament of resilience. It's a gift to witness you reclaim your joy and step into the light of who you truly are. Keep going—because the world is brighter with you in it, fully alive and open to love once more.

105

Angel Message of the Day

Compassion is the soul's way of remembering that we're all walking each other home—each of us navigating this sacred, messy, beautiful human experience with hearts that have known both ache and wonder. It's the grace to look beyond the surface and see the tender truth in one another's eyes, to recognize the silent battles, the quiet courage, the unspoken dreams. True compassion says, "I see your humanity, I feel your spirit, and I'm cheering for you with all my heart." It's the divine thread that weaves us together, reminding us that we don't have to journey alone—and that love, in its purest form, is walking beside one another with open hearts and unwavering Presence.

106

*Y*ou Are Capable

You are capable beyond your wildest dreams—more powerful, more resilient, and more gifted than you've ever been told. Your ability is the foundation, the raw potential within you, waiting to be fully realized. Your motivation is the spark that drives you forward, fueled by purpose, passion, and the whisper of your soul's calling. But it's your attitude—your belief in yourself, your willingness to rise after setbacks, your choice to see possibility—that shapes how brightly you shine. When these three align, there is nothing you cannot create, become, or overcome. You were made for greatness—now it's time to believe it.

*T*he Eternal Gift

One of the greatest gifts you can give someone is to help them find their way back to themselves—to gently remind them of who they are beneath the noise, the wounds, and the weight they've carried for too long. It's not about fixing or saving them, but about holding up a mirror to their soul so they can remember their light, their strength, and their truth. When you offer this kind of love—the kind that sees, believes, and reflects— you're not just supporting someone, you're helping them return home to the deepest, most sacred parts of who they are. And that is a gift that echoes far beyond this lifetime.

108

*T*rue Freedom

In the moment you release the outcome of what you thought "it should look like," you gift yourself something priceless—freedom. Freedom to breathe, to expand, to allow life to unfold in ways more beautiful and aligned than you could have ever planned. By surrendering the need to control the path, you open the door to miracles, redirections, and divine timing. You no longer limit your future to a single picture; instead, you invite countless possibilities to rise and meet you. Trust that what's meant for you will never miss you— and that sometimes, the greatest blessings arrive wrapped in the unexpected.

*T*his Life Is Sacred

You have been waiting lifetimes to be this version of you—the one who carries the wisdom of the past, the strength born from every soul lesson, and the light that only you can shine. This moment, this you, is sacred. Don't waste it doubting your worth or shrinking to fit into places you've outgrown. You are the culmination of so much love, growth, and divine timing. Stand tall in your truth, speak from your soul, and live like you were meant to—boldly, bravely, and beautifully. This is the lifetime your soul has been preparing for.

.

110

You Aren't Lost

You aren't lost—you're in the sacred in-between, the tender space where transformation is quietly unfolding. Your old self has outgrown its form, and your new self is still gathering strength, wisdom, and wings. It's uncomfortable because you're shedding layers that no longer serve you, making space for the version of you that is more aligned, more authentic, and more free. This is not the end—it's the becoming. Trust this beautiful chaos, for within it lies the miracle of your rebirth.

111

Expect Miracles

Expect miracles and magic in this life – not as rare events, but as your soul's natural rhythm. The Universe is constantly conspiring in your favor, weaving beauty into ordinary moments and placing divine alignments in your path. When you open your heart, you begin to see it: the right words at the right time, the unexpected blessing, the feeling that you are exactly where you're meant to be. This life is not meant to be dull or heavy – it's meant to remind you of the wonder you carry and the love that surrounds you. Trust it. Expect it. Miracles are not coming – they are already here.

Michelle Clare is a multifaceted practitioner with an abundance of spiritual expertise. As a Certified Medium, Angel Intuitive, and Spiritual Coach, she navigates the realms beyond our physical existence. Additionally, Michelle brings her gifts as a Medical Intuitive and Energetic Healer to illuminate the paths of healing and self-discovery. Having survived three Near Death Experiences and having had three Shared Death Experiences—Michelle's journey is marked by resilience and profound transformation. Michelle is excited to share new information about Soul Plans, Shared Death Experiences, and navigating the delicate landscape surrounding suicide.

You can connect with her on Instagram, Facebook, and YouTube by visiting her website at www.michelleclare.net

www.ingramcontent.com/pod-product-compliance
Lightning Source LLC
Chambersburg PA
CBHW021117130626
46554CB00002B/746